ALL THE WORKPLACE IS A STAGE:
Acting Techniques to Create Award-Winning Business Performance

LINDA SHERWIN

This book is dedicated to five wonderful men in my life.

To Gerald Sherwin, my father, from whom I received the entrepreneurial flair for doing it my way and whose passing at 91 years was far too soon.

To Randall, my brother, who has been one of my best friends for a very long time.

To Andrei, my son, who at five years old thought his Mom was cool and still does these many years later.

To Grayson and Rhys, my grandsons, whose arrival in this world gave me the courage to get back up and the fortitude to keep on going.

To Genina Perfetti Sherwin, my mother, who has always had and still has a phenomenal voice, and although she never had the chance to present it on the world stage, she sings in the hearts of all who know her.

"All the world's a stage and all the men and women merely players. They have their exits and their entrances; And one man in his time plays many parts."

William Shakespeare, 1599
As You Like It – Act II, Scene VII

"All the workplace is a stage and every player must know his or her role, and be passionately involved in the outcome of the performance of the organization."

Linda Sherwin, 2006

Contents

Acknowledgments

There were many wonderful people who helped me to create and finish this book.

To Mary and Tony Dionisi at whose wedding I received my first applause many years ago,

To Lisa Bell and my colleagues at the Florida Speakers Association and the National Speakers Association who first encouraged me to do it,

To Anna Beach and JoAnn Smalarz for their unending support and Friday-night margaritas to help the creative process,

To the Nomads Acting Group and Peter Hall's Theater of Dreams for giving me a wealth of performances to call upon,

To Gerri Sefi and Cindy Kemp for their encouragement and Friday-night wine to help the creative process,

To Cousin Jan Neundorf, who in the final days gave tremendous assistance and kept me laughing,

To Laura Brandes, my interview partner and friend,

To my son Andrei for the creative cover design,

To the many new social media contacts who gave their opinions and support,

To Anne McIndoo, who started me on this book journey, and to Alicia Dunams and her team who helped me to finish it,

And lastly, to Jake and Elwood, my chocolate labs, who laid at my feet wherever I was working and whose calming snores and occasional need for an ear rub kept me sane throughout the process.

Overture

I was four years old and the flower girl in the wedding of family friends. In my baby-blue tiered organza gown, I felt like a princess. Little did I know the "ham" I was to become was born that day as well! For some reason unknown to me then and still to this day, I stood up on a chair at the reception and sang a wedding song to the bride and groom. My mother said it was the most natural thing for me to do.

And then came the applause . . . . . . and I was hooked!

Instead of pursuing performance as a career, I spent over 20 years as a corporate consultant. However, for fun, as a hobby or to satisfy the passion lit that day long ago, I performed in theater productions for many years.

As a consultant, I worked extensively in the areas of process and performance improvement, organizational effectiveness, and communication. For many years, I helped individuals in small, mid-size, and large organizations in public and private sectors in Canada and the USA to identify and tap into their uniqueness and to use authentic communication to achieve success.

I worked with many business people who were having a difficult time. They were working hard and doing the best they could. But they weren't being themselves. They weren't allowed to bring what I call their "uniqueness" to the world. It's a fact that you spend more of your time in the business world and with your business associates than you do with your family. The importance of being authentically *you* in that situation became very evident to me.

Soon, my two passions began to merge. The similarities between a theatrical play and the theater of business are quite interesting and profound. I realized that the elements that create an award-winning play are similar to the elements that create a successful organization. Whether that organization is a small business, a large corporation, or a non-profit association, success depends on a number of factors. And all the factors must be there in order to have the desired result – a long-running play or an ongoing successful business.

I realized it's important that people understand the concept, and I wanted it to be simple. A method that they could "get" and implement immediately.

As I worked with individuals and organizations, a methodology began to unfold – a methodology which can be easily learned, is immediately applicable, and which expedites results. And in 2006, I created the four-step process.

As I started to work this theory into my consulting and speaking business, people began asking me for more specific details on how they could apply this to their business lives. And hence, this book was born!

This book is for anyone who has to communicate...but of course, that's everyone these days, isn't it? We are all communicators. I am focusing on people who are in management positions, directors, or anyone who is in a leadership role. I believe that by starting at the top with managers, directors, C-suite executives, rolling it throughout the whole organization, a momentum is created that is unstoppable.

How does this all translate to you in your workplace and your desire for success? Simply put, in order to be the best you can be, to maximize your performance, and in order to be part of an award-winning company, it is important for every person, every character in the theater of your business to:

- "identify" his authentic role in the organization,
- "project" it through every interaction with everyone she contacts both internally and externally,
- "anchor" that role in a solid foundation, and
- "duplicate" it over and over every day.

Four steps – easy, and it can be simple. I will take you step by step through the process. I ask you to have an open mind in reading this book. Try the exercises and see what results you get.

I know you may say, "But I am a business person; I'm not a performer. How can this work for me?" And I say you <u>are</u> a performer – a star – in <u>your</u> business. Whether you own the business, or are in a leadership or a support position, your performance will have a direct effect on the overall success.

The workplace is indeed a stage and every player must play his or her part.

Remember, the play's the thing!

Be ready for your cue! Hit your mark!

Curtain up! It's show time!

Linda Sherwin
August 2014

Prologue

The Nightmare

This is it! You are totally prepared.

Your wardrobe has been painstakingly assembled to perfection. Your accessories have been carefully chosen to complement your ensemble. You are primed in every way.

You are totally confident in what you have to say and how to say it. You have practiced every aspect of this time and time again.

The audience is ready with silence and eager anticipation.

You stand behind the curtain waiting for the correct moment.

Now. You stride onto the stage resplendent in your Shakespearean attire. As you open your mouth to begin the well-rehearsed soliloquy, all the others in perfect harmony break into a roaring rendition of "Five hundred twenty-five thousand six hundred minutes!"[1]

You have a gut-wrenching feeling of surprise, fear, and utter dismay. "Oh no! I'm in the wrong play!"

Whether in business or life – it's happened to you. **The Actor's Nightmare.** That horrific moment when you realize you are the wrong person in the wrong place at the wrong time.

"The Play's the Thing"

Hamlet – Act II Scene II

Your Business is Important

The Actor's Nightmare. The wrong person in the wrong place at the wrong time. Is this how you feel in your organization? Is there a misfit or disconnect between you and what you want to do and what is really going on around you?

If you are in a leadership position, is this possibly the reason that your company is not doing as well as you would like? If you are in a support position, is this possibly the reason that you are not advancing as far or as quickly as you would like?

In order to answer these questions, let's take a look at why I chose a theater analogy for this book.

When my two passions – consulting and theater – began to merge, the similarities were staring me in the face. As an actor, you have to convince the audience that you are a particular character. You have to create the character in their mind, build the characterization and elicit the relationship you want to achieve toward that character. Do you want the audience to like the character or not, have sympathy for him or not, want revenge for her or against her? You have to create interest in the character's outcome, leave the audience with a lasting impression and entertain them, all in the matter of a couple of hours. That's quite an achievement when you think about it.

As a leader in your particular workplace on your stage, what character are you portraying? What particular role have you chosen to play or have you even made a conscious choice? You really need your "audience," your people, to see you as that leader. You have to have your people see who you really are, respect you, and understand what you are trying to achieve. You might say, "Of course the message gets across!" Yes, the message may be heard, but is it accepted and acted upon with the enthusiasm and commitment that is required to really make it work?

Your people also have to understand what their part is in the business and be motivated to be engaged and fulfill their duty in the day-to-day strive for success. Just as an actor convinces the audience of who they are and gets the audience involved in the action of the play. That's what a leader has to do in an organization.

Let's take a look at a theater production. It takes a large group of people, many who are behind the scenes, to create a successful play. When Hamlet is offered a goblet of poisoned wine by Horatio, the goblet is physically there because of the diligence of the prop master. When the scenery changes easily from one locale to another, it does so through the efforts of the stagehands. When an actor convincingly portrays a character, a lot of credit belongs to the makeup and costume assistants. So while none of these people are ever seen, nor get the applause they rightly deserve, they are an integral part of the success of the performance.

The same applies to the theater of business. Where would the business be without the cheerful and professional receptionist, the meticulous and attentive administrative assistants, or the dependable and diligent customer-service staff? While their responsibility is not to create policy and processes, it is because they implement and carry out these directives that the business thrives.

Of course, everyone in a play is working from the same script. What chaos would ensue onstage if that were not the case? And what of the audience? Are they getting what they expected and what they paid for? They would have no idea what they were seeing, would probably remain for only a short time, and then leave and ask for their money back.

What about your audience, your clients, and customers? Do they see a cohesive group of people working towards the same common purpose? Do they see everyone playing their vital role as well as they can? And because of that, are they more inclined to stay, tell others they know, and perhaps come back again?

And why did I choose to relate this process to William Shakespeare?

Shakespeare's memorable words were written over 400 years ago, world-renowned and translated into every language. Unbeknownst to many people, his words are still popular today. Some expressions used in day-to-day conversation are based on Shakespeare. Have you ever said any of the following expressions?

Bated breath	Break the ice
Dead as a doornail	Full circle
Good riddance	In a pickle
Lie low	Melted into thin air
Not slept one wink	Own flesh and blood
Seen better days	Spotless reputation
There's no such thing	Too much of a good thing
What's done is done	Wild goose chase

If so, you have been quoting William Shakespeare. And these are but a few of the expressions that are still used today. What a phenomenal business it would be to have that longevity, breadth, depth, and popularity!

And why a theater analogy, as opposed to a television or media one? In theater, you have one chance to make that first impression. No matter how many rehearsals and practices you have, once the curtain goes up, it literally is show time! There are no re-takes or do-overs. If something goes wrong, the actors on the stage must continue to play their characters and continue the storyline for the sake of the audience. And everything flows from start to finish. Both movies and television allow re-takes over and over again if need be. Often, they are not filmed in order, for logistics of lighting or make-up or any other number of reasons.

In business, you rarely get a chance to have a "do-over." In today's competitive global market, if you make a mistake with a client or customer, they have any number of other places to go to get the same product or service. Members of your staff have other opportunities as well, and they can leave if they don't feel they are working in a company that suits them or where they have a "fit."

In the 2013 State of the Global Workplace report by Gallup, a well-respected, research-based global performance-management consulting company, it stated that in 142 companies worldwide, the number of employees truly engaged in their jobs was only 13%.[2] What does this do to the productivity of these companies? A November 2011 worldwide study by Mercer, the large New York City-based human resources consulting firm, reported that between 28–56% of employees expressed a desire to leave their jobs.[3] Although these people are staying in their jobs for the moment, are they really involved and contributing all that they can? In the summer of 2012, in a national Canadian survey, IPSOS Reid, one of the world's leading survey-based marketing research firms, reported that 61% of the Canadian workforce say they don't trust their senior leaders, "don't believe what leaders are saying," and do not think that senior leadership is doing a good job in communicating what is happening in their workplace.[4]

Are these leaders the wrong people in the wrong place at the wrong time?

"To Thine Own Self Be True"

Hamlet – Act I Scene III

Your Authenticity

A s an actor, you have a responsibility to the author of the character and to the director's interpretation of it. In life, your responsibility is to yourself. How true are you to yourself? As Shakespeare said in *Hamlet*, "To thine own self, be true." Most of us are familiar with that particular phrase, but how many people know the rest of the verse? "And it must follow as the night the day, thou cannot be false to any man." What does that mean? Unless we can be true to ourselves first, we cannot be true to others. This is the first step in really connecting and communicating with people – knowing yourself and being true to who you really are.

Sure, you may think that you know who you are. In fact, when someone says to you, "Introduce yourself," how many times have you told them what you <u>do</u>? You're a vice president. You're a manager. You're a sales rep. Depending on whom you're talking to, perhaps you'll describe yourself in a more personal way. You're a father. Perhaps you'll tell them the number of children you have or where you have originally come from. Does that really define who <u>you</u> are?

When you really think of it, we all have a lot of personalities. Both in business and in our personal lives, we wear a lot of hats, and for each hat, we assume a lot of identities. Which one is the identity that is closest to who we really are? Are we aware of which identity we are using in a particular situation? And is it appropriate for that precise moment?

Returning to the theater analogy, think of what an actor has to do. An actor goes through an initial process in order to find the identity of the character that he is about to play. There is the "character analysis" in order to find the true characterization needed for the role. Using a popular process based on the techniques originally created by Constantin Stanislavski in the early 1900s, some actors draw on their own emotions and memories to bring authenticity to the roles.

In order to bring that realism to your role in business, it is important to identify it. So it is essential to find out, first of all, who "you" are. Once you know who you are, then you are able to use the real "you" to take on the required identity – the authentic identity – that's required for the particular situation that you are in.

Why is it important to know who you are? What are the benefits of knowing who you really are? In my work as a consultant, I realized that there were a lot of people who were unhappy at their work. They just weren't doing what it was they wanted to do. In most cases, when you asked them, they simply said they didn't know what it was they wanted to do. That stems from not knowing who they were, so when they communicated with people, that feeling or lack thereof was coming across and being interpreted in many – and usually negative – ways.

Most people really know who they are instinctively, at some level. How you know is because when you're there it feels good. It resonates with you, so you know at some point, who you are. Who you are will make you feel passionate. It will light you up. It gets you excited. It will make you feel that you are really being "you."

One way of checking it out is to listen to what you say when you talk to yourself – I call it "mind chatter." It's those times that your mind is racing away, talking. Listen to what it has to say. Actors will use that to put themselves into a state, to make sure that they have the characterization correct, by creating the character and then listening to what that character – not the actor – is saying to them as they play the role.

Do other people around you know who you really are? As a business person, of course, people will know your name, your business title, and what perhaps you are doing, but do they really know who you are? Do you allow them to see the real you? Again, it must start with you knowing who the real you is.

Do you change dramatically according to the situation? Does that mean that people in business would not be sure how you might respond when they approach you? Or, are you playing so many different roles that people cannot relate to you because they do not know who the real you is?

As a business person, you know who you are. You know your title and your rank in the organization, but what would be a word that might describe you in a particular situation? It's sometimes "powerful," and another time it's "accommodating," and maybe another time, it's "successful" or "profitable" or "triumphant." Be conscious of how you want to be at any time in the day. Deliberately focus on that one word that describes you and with a little patience, you can immediately be that character.

I'm not suggesting that you be false or phony in any way; all these characteristics are really a part of who you are. You simply need to emphasize that particular characteristic at any particular moment. Just because you're a C-suite executive doesn't mean that you can't be "compassionate," and just because you're an administrative assistant doesn't mean that you can't be "powerful." There are times when each of these characters will need to be something that is not typical for them. It's about knowing that you have these characteristics and can call upon them at any time.

Perhaps you've never really experienced having that characteristic, or perhaps you've never allowed people to see that in you. It takes focus and consciousness, just like it does for an actor. Perhaps an actor is not used to being funny or being dramatic, but by creating the character, doing the characterization and working on it, and bringing that character to life every single time they have to, every single time they step onto the stage, they are able to do it over and over and over again. In the same way, you can bring the necessary identity to life whenever you need to.

What are the benefits of finding the real you? First of all, it provides a baseline for you to work from. From this point onward, knowing who you are will allow you to take on the characteristics you need and be authentic in doing so. Other people know when you're not being authentic. You yourself talk to people or hear them communicating with you, and you just know that it's not them being who they really are. The words may say one thing, but you can tell from their nonverbal communication – their voice and body language – that they really mean something else. If you are really you, if you are being truly you, then that will certainly be noticed. The authenticity will be there at any point in time.

You may find that the best role to use is not necessarily one you might have thought of in a particular situation. The voice that you would use talking to a young child is very different than the voice that you would use in giving business instructions to someone. However, if you are explaining a new process to an associate, you would provide each step required, which has some similarities to explaining something to a young child. It's important that in your role you step back and understand that it is something new and different, and you want to be sure he fully understands. You might ask him questions afterwards to ensure his comprehension. You may also find that you are more empathetic and more careful of the words you use. You may actually be calling upon several roles already within you. Knowing that these roles are within you and that they are appropriate in the business world can be very useful.

Using this technique, you will also feel extremely fulfilled because you'll be satisfying the person inside of you. You'll be feeling that you are being authentic and real to yourself, as well as to other people. That's a truly fulfilling experience for you. So many people today are not fulfilled, and I believe it's because they're not being who they really are. By being who you really are, you certainly will feel content. You'll be much more efficient and effective at what you're doing because again, it will resonate with you, and that authenticity will resonate with other people. Again, knowing who you are allows you to work more effectively in business, and it will relate to your personal life as well.

When you are being real and true to yourself, you'll make

better choices. You'll find that you'll make better decisions in your business and in your personal life as well. When an actor embodies the character that they have chosen to be and really, truly becomes that character, they're no longer acting. They are actually "being" the character, and the choices that they make will be real and true to that character. Once you know who you are, you will be real and true to your character, which is the real "you."

When you see a well-played character in a performance, ask yourself why you no longer see the actor, only the character they portray? It's that authenticity, the fact that the actor is no longer an actor, but is being the character. The character is real. What about you? Are you being real in your communications?

"To Be or Not To Be"

Hamlet – Act III Scene I

The Choices You Make

T he answer to the question "to be or not to be" is simple – BE! Be you in the best way possible for the situation you are in, for the role you are in. I've always thought the word "acting" was a misnomer because really great actors don't "act" – they actually "be" the character, and do it in such a profound way that, as the observer, you no longer see the actor but rather the character they are portraying. One of the first lessons of acting is to "be in the moment," which simply means as the character you must do, say, feel, and respond as the character would in that moment. If something goes wrong during a stage production and the actor is truly "in the moment," she will respond as the character would and continue the performance. Remember there are no do-overs in a live production. In business, when something goes wrong, do you and your people continue to perform as expected?

The first step in the process is IDENTIFY. This is the most important step in the process – to identify the roles you perform in your life. This is the foundation.

You may ask, "Do I have to be an actor?" And the answer is "No, you don't." Because we are communicating all the time, we are in roles all the time. It's important to know the role that we are in at a given time and what the most acceptable role is for the particular situation that we're in.

For instance, I personally am a daughter, a sister, a mother, an aunt, a grandmother, a cousin, and a great aunt. I'm also a gardener, a dog-walker, a dancer, a friend, and a confidante. As a businessperson, I am a consultant, a speaker, an author, and a coach. Because I have my own business, I am also a sales rep, a marketing rep, a web-content creator, and bookkeeper. I could go on and on and on. I have a lot of different roles that I play, and in each role, I am authentically ME.

I've often said in my workshops that the role that I play as a grandmother playing dragons on the floor with my grandchildren is very different than the role that I play as a businessperson talking in a conference room to a group of executives. Although, I sometimes wonder if maybe the role of playing dragons on the floor might be more effective with the executives!

But all of those roles are real, and they are all me. I choose to play a different role depending on the situation that I'm in. Some are conscious choices at the time, and some are simply an unconscious but learned reaction to the moment. You have all sorts of different roles, and you do play them all – and you play them all authentically, but you choose to play different ones at different times in your life, in different relationships in your life, and even at different moments in your day. The important point is knowing when to play which role.

In the same way that an actor works hard in the initial steps of preparation so that she can *be* the character in the moment, it's important and advantageous for you to identify your roles and when to play each one so that you can be very authentic in the moment. With that authenticity, you are seen by others in the best light. You actually become very powerful because it's you, and the real you is very passionate! That passion is very effective, and it will lead to your success. Think about it. Do you know any successful person who is not passionate about what she does? Passion is critical to your success.

How do people determine their roles? It's simple, but not necessarily easy. The first exercise is to brainstorm, and you write down all of the roles that you play. (You can download the workbook to use at lindasherwin.com/WorkplaceWorkbook.html, where I have provided some suggestions to get you started.) To identify as many as possible, you need to take the time as you go through your day to mark down the roles you are playing. Do it as you go through your business day and as you go through your personal day. Go through every aspect of your life. You might be a sports person and also a philanthropist who works with charities. You may be a businessperson who enjoys painting or another creative endeavor. This list-making takes a little time but is fundamental to the process. Often people are quite surprised when they realize the various roles that they play.

So often in life we are defined by what we <u>do</u>. How often have you said to somebody, "Who are you?" and he'll say, "Well, I am a Senior Manager of XYZ Company." They will define themselves according to that one role, yet they have all sorts of other roles that are really them as well, and perhaps they don't see the importance of that. For example, sometimes as the Senior Manager, it's important that you be a little more creative in order to work out a problem. Or perhaps, you many have a little bit more empathy, and that may come from a different part of you, a different role that you wouldn't necessarily associate with your usual business role.

What can happen if you use the wrong or an inappropriate "you" in a situation? Your role plays a large part in conveying your message, and the message could be misinterpreted or received badly. Knowing your roles, how you portray them, and how to recall them is what this process is all about.

So the first step in identifying the roles that you play is literally to write them down. Just make a list and it becomes the foundation for the next steps. How vital are each of those roles to your success? You might be very surprised. For instance, I said that I walk my own dogs. Is that a role that has skills that might be valuable in business? There just might be. If I am walking my dogs, and they see another dog and start to pull and get rambunctious, what do I have to do? Do I first assess the situation to see if there is any risk in approaching the other dog? Do I proceed to let them interact, or do I give a command to "sit and stay" and let the other dog go past? Those are skills that I have that are transferable, perhaps, to another role that I play.

That's what an actor does. In working on a role, he takes the experiences that he has and brings them to that particular character. So start off by simply identifying all of the roles that you play. Give different names to the roles on the list that will make sense to you. The more you personalize this, the better.

Once you have identified each role, the next step is to determine all the characteristics of the role. This will also take some time. Just as an actor determines all aspects of the character she is about to portray, it is important to consciously define all the characteristics of each role that you play — both positive and negative. Use the workbook to list as many characteristics as you can. If you are not sure in which column to put a characteristic, put it in both. After all, there may be times when being a confidante might be positive and other times it might be negative. List as many characteristics as possible and use whatever means necessary to call them to mind. You might get ideas from books, movies, or everyday life.

This first step is the foundation of the process. You may find that you go back to this list and add identities and characteristics as they occur. The importance of "being" has to start with finding out who you are as a particular character, so that you can draw on that part of you when needed.

ACT III SCENE I
"Well We Shall See Your Bearing"
The Merchant of Venice – Act II Scene II

How Others See You

In Shakespeare's *The Merchant of Venice*, Bassanio admonishes his friend, Gratiano, to conduct himself properly. Otherwise, people will get the wrong impression of both of them. He tells Gratiano, "Well, we shall see your bearing." In other words, "We'll see how you act."

Shakespeare knew the value of an impression and how it was communicated. He was making a valid point over 400 years ago that is still true today.

Communication is what we are really talking about when it comes to empowering staff or maintaining loyal customers. We have discussed finding the right identity for you to be in various situations, and the way that identity is presented is through communication. In the same way that an actor learns her lines, gestures, and the use of props to communicate the characterization, a business leader needs to know the importance of all aspects of communication, and to understand the value of effective communication and the dangers of miscommunication.

People do it all the time. You are always communicating something to someone whether you realize it or not. Whether you are talking to a colleague or a friend, using some sort of technology, or simply walking around, you are communicating and telling people either what you need, what you are doing, or what you are thinking.

In every communication, there are three parts:
- The sender.
- The message.
- The recipient of the message.

Any one of those steps can make a huge difference in what happens after the communication takes place. It's important that people understand that they are communicating all the time, and for every communication, there will always be a result. Some results may be good, some results terrible, and others somewhere in between, but there will always be a result to every communication that occurs.

People communicate in a variety of ways. They can talk to each other, whether it is face-to-face or by using a device. People communicate nowadays through e-mails and through social media. People communicate simply by how they look: their faces, their tone of voice, and their body language – all aspects of communication that affect the results.

There are times when people are not aware that they are communicating. (Apparently, I talk in my sleep, so I'm definitely communicating all the time.) Many of us forget that, even if no one is around, and you're all by yourself – whether driving, walking along, or sitting quietly – you have "mind chatter," those internal conversations with ourselves that speed through our minds, ever-changing throughout the day. Attributed to the National Science Foundation, a U.S. government agency that supports research in the biological sciences, among other disciplines, the average person is reported to have as many as 50,000 thoughts per day.[5] Those thoughts, or chatter, can be positive or negative, and they have an unconscious but direct effect on how you are outwardly perceived. We've all experienced seeing a friend or colleague who looks to be in a very bad mood, only to realize that the drive to work was fraught with bad weather or crazy drivers. You can be sure that he had numerous conversations with himself about the state of the day or the other drivers.

The phenomenon can be far more encompassing than simply being in a bad mood. Although the name of the author seems to be in dispute, the essence of the words is evident:

"Watch your thoughts, for they become words.
Watch your words, for they become actions.
Watch your actions, for they become habits.
Watch your habits, for they become character.
Watch your character, for it becomes your destiny."

The Latin root for communication means "to impart, to share or to make common" and was originally related to gifts or duties, and not the human connection involved in speaking or reading.[6] Therefore, if you think of communication as a gift, the reasons for communication are numerous – to inspire, to share an idea, to compliment, or to explain. There are various reasons to communicate, and there will always be a result.

People communicate everything. They communicate emotions, ideas, requests, or commands. People communicate to negotiate, to argue, to inspire, to motivate, or to convince. Every time we deal with someone else, or even with ourselves, we are communicating.

In this book, I've chosen to focus specifically on verbal communication – the communication that happens either face-to-face or when using a device such as a cell phone. Verbal communication is one of the major forms of communication today, and yet, with all of the new technological ways to communicate (text, social media, or e-mail), have we lost the ability to actually talk to people?

Miscommunication can happen for any number of reasons because of the three parts to it – sender, message, and recipient – and any one of the steps can easily create a problem. If the sender uses a certain tone of voice, or particular words, or looks a particular way when they are giving that verbal communication, the meaning can be critically altered. The message may be the same, but those other aspects of the communication will make a huge difference in how it is received by the recipient.

If the recipient doesn't receive the message correctly, then the result won't be there – and that's one of the biggest challenges I have found in business. If the communication is not received properly, then the result that the person or organization is looking for won't happen.

Some studies have shown that with any communication, the impact of the message is based 7% on the words used, 38% on the voice, and 55% on the body language of the sender.[7] When it comes to a face-to-face message, the impact of the nonverbal portion is huge. For people who are talking over the phone, the effect of their voice is magnified to 86% because only your voice is being heard.[8] The message recipient is not able to see your facial expressions or body movements, but these normally make a huge difference in your voice and how it is heard.

People usually think that <u>what</u> they have to say is most important. Making a presentation, leading a meeting, or setting up a project team, many leaders will simply provide the necessary information and think that is sufficient. They forget the rest of the message impact – not just the words that they use, but <u>how</u> they do it and <u>where</u> they do it. Do the leaders simply pull everyone into a conference room and tell them what it is that they want to have done? Have they done anything in advance to allow others to share their ideas?

Even Shakespeare, with the longevity of his works, often uses soliloquies to allow the audience to "hear" the musings of the character. However, his characters have to communicate to each other to move the story or plotline along. The same is true in business. No one can read your mind. Are you giving a complete communication so that there will be no chance of misunderstanding?

Let's go back to the Latin root for "communicate," which means "to make common." If all I am doing is talking <u>at</u> my people, there isn't really a commonality to it, I'm only expressing my way. "Making common" means that both parties must have input into it. One of the biggest outcomes in a miscommunication is where leaders in organizations simply give orders and expect the people to follow through. Communication really should be a two-way street.

Having spent a number of years as a corporate consultant, I was often involved in projects that had to do with change management – where changes were being implemented that meant people were going to be doing things in a new way. In many instances, I found that it wasn't so much the *change* that people resented, rather, it was actually the way it was *communicated* to them. As a result, those people had the power to sabotage the changes, whether it was consciously or not. In the 2012 Canadian study I mentioned earlier, conducted by Ipsos Canada, if results said 61% of the Canadian workforce said they don't believe what their leaders say,[9] how receptive would these people be to change in the organization? If there is no trust that the leaders are doing the right thing, people might not do what they are asked to do, or they do it begrudgingly or incorrectly, simply because of the way it was communicated to them. I found that the way information was given to people, the way it was told to them, made a huge difference in what the results were, how the people responded to the particular communication, how well they actually did it, and how they felt about doing it. Either way, the end result has a direct effect on the success of the company.

As I said, in any communication you are going to have results – good, bad, or somewhere in between. People are going to respond to the way they receive the communication. How do you know if your message has been received properly? One of the benefits of learning about this process is that you learn how to read other people. I'm sure you've been in the middle of a communication when suddenly, you realize someone isn't listening.

How do you know? There may be physical signs – they look away or they fidget with something. Or it might be a facial expression of eyes roaming or a yawn. Nowadays people look at their cell phones almost constantly. Are they giving you the attention you need? If not, use one of your identities to get them back on board without specifying the individual in a group. If need be, ask a question to check in with them. Actors have had to improvise on stage on occasion to get another actor back on track without the audience realizing it.

So if something is miscommunicated, any number of things could happen. What are the problems when a miscommunication results in a process being handled incorrectly? Could it be that time and money have to be spent to re-do goods or services? Is a customer going to be upset and switch to your competition? Is it possible that your best employees find somewhere else to work? Any of those results – losing valuable employees, a decrease in productivity, losing customers – are all going to affect a company's bottom line. So the importance of communication is critical.

How serious could the results of a miscommunication or bad communication be? I will share a story that happened a number of years ago. I had a 12-month consulting contract for an American start-up company. When I first began the project, they wanted to get some processes in place and to set things up properly. There was only about 21 people on the staff at the time. It was a great technical company, amazing product, and wonderful people. The owner/president of the company was a brilliant technical man but was rather distant and impersonal, difficult to approach. The company grew very quickly, and in a short time, the staff had just under 100 people. So they'd gone from 21 people to 100 people in less than a year.

Around this time, a senior person, a vice president, was hired. The president had the utmost trust in the new hire and truly believed he was the right person to help the company grow even more. Unfortunately, the man was a terrible communicator. He gave orders; it was all one-way. There was no commonality to the communication. He spoke in a harsh voice. He always had a very physical demeanor of being in charge, and everyone had to do things his way. Everything about him made it very difficult for people to work with him. He became the link between everyone else in the office and the president. His communication with the president was very different than that with the staff. Because the president was difficult to approach and there was now a blockade to get to him, the staff had no recourse but to put up with the situation or leave. Gradually, people began to leave. Really good and extremely talented people left the company. It was like watching a giant snowball roll down a hill, destroying everything in its path, and there was nothing anyone could do.

About six months after my contract was over, I learned that the business was almost gone. There were 24 employees left. By the time the owner realized what was wrong, it was too late. He had lost all his good people. The customers had left; productivity was down. A short while later, the company closed. All because of one person who communicated very, very badly and had a huge effect on the entire company.

It's critical when undertaking the process to improve communication to start at the very top of the organization and have it filter through to all levels. Buy-in from the C-suite executives who begin to practice the technique becomes almost infectious – in a good way! – within the organization. The authenticity becomes evident with peers, staff members, customers, and vendors. There is no question or second-guessing as to what is meant or required.

Let's just look at an example. If you're my boss and you say something to me, but there is little or no authenticity to the communication, my thought process might be something like this: "She is saying that to me; however, something doesn't seem right. So does she mean that, or does she mean something else? Is she saying that because she wants to alarm me? Is she saying that because she wants to encourage me? Is she saying that because she really means something else and wants me to understand what the other thing is that she wants?" If that's the message I get, how do I respond back? Do I respond back because I believe exactly what you said? Do I respond back thinking that you have a hidden message? Do I hear a mixed message and become confused and frustrated?

You see that miscommunication can have critical results because the recipient of the message is not sure what to do. How does that person respond to the message? Do they respond in a positive way? Do they respond in a negative way? Do they not respond at all? That's the critical aspect of the wrong message being received because you're not going to get the results that you want.

It's so important to be real and authentic in all communications. This four-step process does just that. It teaches you to be an authentic communicator, and once that starts to filter through the organization, all levels have a complete understanding of themselves and each other. Your people understand that you are authentic; they are authentic back to you. They are real and authentic with their customers, and consequently, you have a level of trust that makes for a very successful company.

I call it "full communication." When people do those exercises, they realize the impact of the tone of your voice, facial expressions, and body language. The recipient is receiving everything – the full communication of that message. As leaders, you are being watched by your people, and as noted earlier, you are communicating all the time. Think of it this way, if you have your executives and managers communicating effectively and honestly with their people, the people certainly feel more open. They feel that they can talk about things.

Very often, the director of a play will have the actors work on their characterizations and then see what they bring to the first reading of the play. While the ultimate responsibility lies with the director, she is often open to the actors' interpretation of a particular role or scene because of the authenticity that the actor can bring to it.

When I was doing change management, I found some of the best ideas came from the people who were actually doing the work. This was true in both product- and service-based businesses. The people who were doing the day-to-day work were the ones who really had the great ideas. But they had to feel that it was safe for them to give the ideas to their supervisors or to the management and that the ideas would be openly received and appreciated. When an organization has authentic communication, and people understand that it's okay to present a new idea, even though the company has been doing something one particular way for 20 or 30 years, the results could be amazing. Now you have employees feeling very responsible, feeling very honest, and knowing they can talk about things to their management. They in turn will then be that way with the customers. They're going to do whatever they can to keep the customers loyal to your business.

This step in the process is best summed up in a quote by Ralph Waldo Emerson: "Who you are speaks so loudly that I can't hear what you are saying."

ACT III SCENE II
"Yet There Is Method In It"
Hamlet – Act II Scene II

Using Full Communication

I n Shakespeare's *Hamlet*, Polonius speaks these words in an aside to the audience, questioning whether Hamlet is actually insane or is acting that way on purpose. Was Hamlet choosing to walk, talk, and act that way for a reason? <u>You</u> should be choosing to walk, talk, and act in a certain way to characterize your role.

The next step in the process is PROJECT. As mentioned earlier, this is "full communication" and using all aspects of your character to send your message – your words, voice, and body language. When it comes to being authentic in this full communication, everything comes into play. And you only have a short time to present yourself. Whether a vendor, a customer, or anyone doing business with you, the first impression of you or your company can be critical to your success. Your customer service rep might lose your most important client. Your receptionist might be your best sales rep. One of my clients had a plaque made for the reception desk of the company. It read "Director, First Impressions." How very true. Studies have stated that you have anywhere from one-tenth[10] of a second to seven[11] seconds to make a first impression. Whatever the actual number is, two things are true: it happens very quickly, and you won't get a second chance to make a first impression!

This is what an actor does. There are numerous ways for an actor to approach characterization, and they must find the way that works for them, just as you must find the way that works for you. Some actors have to find how a character walks. Others need to find how they hold their body. Others need to find certain props that personify the particular character. Sometimes it's a case of working from the "inside out" and sometimes from the "outside in."

When it's time for you to communicate, do you look, act, and move like the character you are trying to be? It's sometimes easier for people to work from the "outside in." In other words, walking and talking like the person brings the character to life. Most importantly, to allow the successful person to emerge, you must be comfortable with who you are. Working from the "outside in" can be very powerful. As you start to look, act, and move like the successful person, you'll make the choices that will bring you closer to that goal. At each step of the way, ask yourself, "How would this character behave in this particular situation? How would the character respond to that particular question?"

As they often say in acting classes, know the details, be in the moment, and the rest will come. Become conscious of the effect that that has on the people around you. Be consistent with who you are. Again, the importance of knowing who you are so that you can actually work on this. Always, always, be there. When you find that character, "be" there.

Working from the "inside out" requires you to decide exactly how that character would think and feel. Going from the "inside out" is the famous process created by Constantin Stanislavski.[12] Actors often complete a lengthy, detailed character study to know how that particular character would act and react. Using that same method, you are able, from the inside, to embody the person, and it will start to appear externally. Some people are unaware or unconscious of the effect that our inner reactions have on our outer world. In fact, as we internalize what goes on around us, it's shown in our body language and in our facial expressions. Whichever method is chosen, It's important for an actor to embody the character as a whole.

When you watch live theater, how are you able to get an impression of the character being portrayed almost immediately? The actor has perfected the characterization by how she talks, walks, gestures, and thinks to have the audience believe in who she is. By "being in the moment," the actor is able to maintain the characterization throughout the play. Even if something goes wrong, the show must go on! In theater, as in business, there are no do-overs.

Let me share an example with you. I was performing in a play that had a very intricate plot. One of the actors unfortunately said the wrong line, and he advanced the whole play by several pages, an act which left out several important plot details. Every actor on stage knew what had happened. They all stayed in character and with some improvisation were able to bring the play back to the point where he realized his mistake, came back around and got the line correctly and the play could continue as written with all the pertinent details. The audience never knew what happened because the audience didn't have the script, and the other actors knew what they had to do to get back on track.

Very often in business, when you are in a communication, no one has your script. Therefore, you can be who you are, say what it is you have to say, and the message will be created. As the author of whatever it is you have to present, you have the script, and you have all the subplots. You know where it is you are going. You have the outcome that you want to achieve, in the same way an actor does when he performs. Although the actor knows how the story is going to end, you may or may not know. The best chance for getting the results you want is to be as authentic as you can. There is a theatrical saying that unless Shakespeare himself is in the audience, no one really knows the exact next line in *Hamlet*.

Being in the moment for an actor and for a businessperson has a lot to do with listening, and that means not just listening to the words, but to the full communication that is presented to you. We often do not listen. We are so concerned with what we have to say next that we completely miss both the verbal and nonverbal parts of the sender's message. Why do we miss it? Remember those 50,000 thoughts that we have each day? They might just be getting in the way.

In business, when you are talking to someone, they may not necessarily know what it is you're going to say, but they will have a sense of it from your tone of voice, facial expressions, and body language. The importance of projecting your message as completely as possible is critical to its acceptance.

Again, think of your reaction to an actor as they enter the stage for the first time and what they have done to create that image. Think of meeting a colleague or a friend and knowing exactly how she is feeling without her saying a word. Something as simple as whether you walk around the office or close yourself in your own area speaks volumes to your people. I'm not suggesting that you skip down the halls – although that might be very interesting! However, do you have a smile on your face and go out of your way to greet people? As a leader, you are communicating to your staff and to your seniors all the time. So communicate what you really want to say!

This process has proven very helpful to people in sales, where it's important to listen because your customer will tell you what it is they want. A sale can be lost so easily, if you go down the wrong path and the customer leaves and goes elsewhere. Sales, of course, are the heart of a business and keep it going. So full communication, authenticity, and good listening skills have a direct effect on the bottom line.

As a business leader, how can you start to put this into practice? Start with yourself. You've identified the roles that you are and looked at the positive and negative characteristics of that role. Using your workbook, my suggestions, and the following breakdowns, add to each role the physical characteristics that would be an outward display of that personality.

Start with the words that you use. As you communicate in that role, are you knowledgeable, using effective words and the right words? Interviewing someone who understands your industry, they understand the acronyms and buzzwords. Speaking to someone who is not familiar with the industry, you may need to use simpler words or provide further explanation. In addition, as we look at today's global marketplace, when we're communicating in business, we may be talking with someone from another country and another culture. Words can mean different things to different people.

Going back to the theater analogy, who is your audience? Have they come to view a drama, comedy, tragedy, romance, or some combination? In business, are you aware of who your audience is? Are you aware of your customers and of, perhaps, cultural differences? If that's the case, are you using words that first of all, they understand, and secondly, are not harmful? Again, different words mean different things to different cultures, so be mindful of that and choose your words with care.

When you're talking face-to-face with people, you will have both the verbal and nonverbal aspects of communication at your disposal – your voice and your body language. Think of your facial expressions, your eye contact, and your gestures as a means to add to your message. Again, in our global marketplace, different cultures view any variations on these as welcoming or repulsive. If your work necessitates working with different cultures or travelling to different countries, you would do well to research acceptable forms of behavior.

Think of the tone of voice that you use. Take a single word – the word "great" – and say it in a number of different ways. Say it so it sounds good. Say it sarcastically, angrily, playfully, with surprise, with boredom, with excitement, and as a question. Just think of it, one word, and the tone of your voice can change the meaning incredibly. The voice you use is an important part of your character for the role. Voice embodies a number of characteristics, including tone, articulation, diction, rhythm, and phrasing. Your tone of voice is a strong indicator of who you are. Would a nasal, raspy, breathy, or strained voice be particularly motivating? Would a strong, smooth voice be more likely to encourage and inspire? Actors use different voices to portray a character more fully, and some actors work only with their voice in voiceover work.

How can you improve your voice? Recording it is one of the easiest ways to hear yourself and work on your voice. However, very few people like the sound of their own voice on a recording. The usual comment is that it does not sound like them – and they are absolutely right. The voice you hear on a recording is not the voice you hear when you speak out loud. Bizarre? Not really. It has to do with vibration.[13]

Try this exercise. Place your hand lightly on your jaw and hum. You'll feel the vibration of the sound in your jaw bone. When we speak, we hear our own voice in two ways. Very slightly and distorted through our ears, but mainly, through the vibration of our skull bones and ear drums, which also gives it a much lower pitch. When we hear our voice on a recording, it usually sounds much higher. A simple way to hear your voice as others do is to cup a hand around each ear and pull your elbows together so they almost touch. In doing so, you have extended your ears and now hear yourself as others do. Do you like how you sound? If you do, that's great. If not, some practice and time can help you improve it. Provided there is not a physical condition, working with a coach or using the exercises in the workbook can make a difference.

Remembering to breathe when you speak is also a good idea. As strange as that may sound, people are often unconsciously holding their breath when they speak until they come to a certain point in their communication. The reason actors can project their voice to the back of the theater is because they have practiced breath control and breathing deeply from the diaphragm. If you are breathing deeply, your stomach area should rise and fall. A simple exercise is to stand with your hands on your stomach. As you breathe in through your nose to a count of five, be conscious of your stomach area expanding, and as you breathe out through your mouth, to a count of ten, allow your stomach to return to its normal position. Do this for a few minutes to become more accustomed to "belly breathing," as it is sometimes called. Controlling your breath will do wonders for improving your voice. Use the workbook to review some exercises to help you become more aware of your voice.

Facial expressions may be large and dramatic or much smaller and shorter – from one-eighth to one-fifth of a second. The latter was termed micromomentary expressions (MME) in 1966 by two researchers, Ernest A. Haggard and Kenneth S. Isaacs.[14] Later in 1969, Dr. Paul Ekman studied microexpressions (brief involuntary expressions of emotion), their use in deception, and then reported the results in the book *Telling Lies* (Ekman, 1985).[15] This was further popularized through the television series *Lie To Me* (2009 – 2011), promoting the concept and leading to friends watching each other with great concentration. Other books and series have amplified the idea that facial expressions can be seen by other people to provide more insight into a communication. At this writing, software has now been developed that can distinguish the tiny changes in facial expressions.[16] For many years, actors have used this technique to add to the characterization of a role. Oftentimes, these expressions would have to be large and dramatic for theater productions, in order for the audience to see it. For your day-to-day communications, your facial expressions can be normal.

Gestures are a big part of nonverbal communication, and like one's voice, they are very different and have different meanings in countries around the world. A well-known gesture in North America may be an insult in other areas. Gestures are used extensively by actors to communicate more fully what their character is thinking, or to provide more insight into the role. Some actors "get into character" by starting with gestures or style of movement as their first step in character analysis. In business, you can use gestures to be more authentic in your characterization or to emphasize certain parts of that character. Other body movements will add to this as well. Your facial expressions and the way you walk, hold your arms, or stand still are all adding to the communication that you are sending.

The recipient's perception of that meaning will change his

interpretation of the message. A person who walks quickly with a long stride may be in a hurry for an important event, or she may be trying to avoid someone or something. A person with tears in his eyes may have just received some bad news, or he may be ecstatically happy. A different emotion can be expressed in the same way by various people because of that particular moment, culture, or a learned behavior. In contrast, the same emotion can be expressed very differently as well. Anger isn't always yelling and screaming. Intense rage might be a clenched jaw and grinding teeth. Grief is not necessarily extreme weeping. Deep anguish might manifest as hysterical laughter.

Mind chatter can add to or detract from your characterization. Those internal conversations can help you to stay in character or can result in a lack of focus. Advertisers use this method in order to get you to buy. The ideas for particular spots can relate to people in such a way that people have an insight; they actually internally feel and understand what is being presented to them. If people can't relate to it, then they either don't care about it or they lose interest, so it's important that as your character, you touch that internal part of people.

As a business person, how do you appear to other people when you communicate? When meeting your prospects for the first time, do you appear confident, successful, sure of your products or services, sure of yourself? How do you appear to the people who work for you or the people to whom you report? What is their impression of you? When you communicate, is their impression the one you are trying to give? Or, have you given them a completely mixed message from what your intention was? Do you have any idea of exactly how that appears to other people? Perhaps you would get better results if you shifted something you were doing. The best way to learn about this is to do it consciously. It sounds like a lot of work, but it is probably something you do every day anyway and are simply not aware of.

People-watch. That's right – observe people around you. I

always suggest that my clients become avid people watchers. Actors do it to create their character more fully. You can do it as well. (Just don't appear as a stalker.) A good place to start is a location of high emotion – perhaps an airport or train station where people may be parting for an emotional reason. Sit yourself in a seat and simply watch.

At an airport, one couple kisses goodbye, and they both cry as he walks to the plane alone. Another couple kisses shyly, and she gives a little wave as she walks to the plane alone. Another couple argues as they walk to the plane together. What are their stories? At a restaurant, a woman laughs hysterically by herself. A man speaks loudly on his cell phone and slams it down on the table. A couple eats in silence, not looking at each other. What is going on in their lives? Watch people, and make up a story to what you see. You may not be correct, and you may never know the true circumstances, but it is your perception of what you have seen that will be your reality.

Notice your response to what you have seen – keeping in mind it is your perception at that particular moment in time. What is going on in your mind or your feelings at the time will make a difference in how you receive the information. Does it make you feel good? Does it make you feel bad? Does it make you feel that you want to help or support? Does it make you feel that you simply want to run away? Is it something you simply wish to avoid? What is your response to it? Your response may be a learned response because of experiences you have had; it would not necessarily be everyone's response to it. There are some almost-universal reactions and responses to certain events, but it doesn't mean that everyone uses them all the time.

Take notes. Write it down. Write what you saw. Write what you thought. Anything that comes to mind – how it made you feel, what was your impression of what was going on? Take your impression at several levels: your emotional response, and also a cerebral one. Be aware of what of yourself you see in the interaction. If you were going through that particular scenario, would you have handled the communication differently? Would you have been different in some way? Not necessarily better or worse, but simply different, and why? Take a look at why you would have responded differently? As you people-watch, what makes you feel good about a person? What puts you off? What would make you reluctant to approach them? Can you tell when they are fearful or when they are worried? As you interact with other people, what makes you feel receptive to what they have to say, to what they have to sell? Is it the words they use, the tone of voice, the body language?

As an actor, one of the best things they do to improve their acting skills is to people-watch. Actors store this information and then call upon it when required to find a character they are playing. No matter what the situation, watch people and see how they respond to their surroundings, to each other, and to themselves. Watch people in a group, in a couple, or alone. It's a wonderful study of people and what makes them be the way they are, as well as how you, the observer, sees them.

Now, turn it around. What are you communicating as a business person? Do you ever question whether someone may be watching you and wondering what is going on in your life? That's right. Everything you do – again, not just the words you use, but every aspect of you – is communicating to those around you. How do you look? What sorts of facial expressions are you making? Where are your eyes focused? What is the tone of your voice? What is your body doing? Is it in agreement with what you are saying or is it, again, giving a mixed message? Keep in mind your nonverbal communication is always there and available for all to see.

As you communicate, be aware of how people are responding to you with their body language. Read in them the potential impression you are making. A person's response to you may depend on something within him. He may have learned reactions based on his past experiences. If he is accustomed to people yelling at him, he might think that a loud voice was yelling and was angry and meant something negative, whereas you might come from a family where talking loudly was simply the way it was done. What impression are you making? It's important for you to be aware of how you are portraying yourself, but also be aware of the person's response to it and learn to read the audience, whether it's one or a hundred, to get a true sense of how they are accepting what it is you have to say.

The benefit of this exercise is to help you to focus on a regular basis in your interactions, no matter how rushed or apparently insignificant they may be. If you are in the moment with the person or people you are with and respond to them authentically and effectively, it will make a big difference in your communications. Others will see you. How others see you will vary. Their impression of you will change, and they will respond to you differently. You will read other people and respond to them effectively. Your communication will be real and will certainly improve because you have taken the time to watch, react, and learn from what is going on. If you are being in the moment, and if you are truly being who you are, then the people you are communicating with will feel the authenticity and will know that is who you really are. You may not know exactly what's going on, but your impression of what is going on is based on what you see, and you will respond accordingly.

It's wonderful to see this process in action. I was working with a small recruiting company that kept a lot of metrics and statistics on their employees. How many people did you interview today? How many jobs did you fill? It was very go, go, go! We started with the executive team and worked with them to have that buy-in and authentic communication start from the very top of the organization. We worked our way down through the management and staff, and it was amazing to watch the transformation. Everyone started to communicate a little differently, especially in the quality of the communications. People were being much more authentic in all aspects of their communication with each other and with their clients. Using "mystery consumers" to assess the progress, we found that the potential clients had a sense of a very professional organization that they wanted to do business with. The staff was courteous and knowledgeable. The metrics and clients increased, and there was an increase in business as well. Great results from improved communication!

It can be helpful in this step of the process to ask for assistance from a trusted friend or colleague. Ask how they see you displaying a variety of moods or emotions and how you look, act, or speak under particular circumstances. By asking people you can trust, it makes it safe and hopefully, honest. People are often amazed at how transparent they are particularly in their nonverbal communications. A clenched jaw or a particular hand gesture tells a big part of the story and may be completely unconscious to you.

Sometimes clients find it difficult to work with people within their own organization, or their friends do not see them in their business setting, so it's difficult to get this feedback. This can create a barrier to their moving forward. In these cases, having them work with somebody that they don't know is still considered safe and gets better results. In the same way that your read of an actor's characterization can happen, the same applies to the business person. What's that first impression you get as she walks into the room? When he's talking and asking questions, what is your sense of his demeanor? Is this someone you like and want to do business with, or do you feel ill at ease and want to end the meeting? What is he doing that makes you feel positive or negative toward him? You may not know exactly what's going on, but your impression of what is going on is based on what you see and your perception of that.

This second step of the process is immediately applicable – PROJECT. You can review the roles you play and determine which aspects of projection will assist you in making the characterization as authentic as possible, in order to be seen as such. Being in the moment creates that authenticity. You will be who you are. You will be consistent. You will be clear. Whoever is dealing with you or listening to you will know exactly what you are talking about. The physical benefit of it is that the body will follow with the appropriate reaction and responses. Be mindful of how you communicate, and as each person starts to do it, it becomes more effective and makes a big positive difference in your organization.

Set aside some time to work on your words and your voice. Go out and people-watch. Initially, a place of high emotion will make it a little easier for you to see the distinct differences. Gradually change your viewing location and try to determine what the everyday person is going through as you simply walk around. Notice people's unusual or non-typical reactions to events. Then, become mindful of your reactions to circumstances and how that may be perceived by others. Be conscious of your facial expressions, tone of voice, body language, and what they portray to the viewer. You never know who is watching you.

ACT IV SCENE I
"Remember Me"
Hamlet – Act I, Scene V

Finding Your Sense Memory

Many years ago, early on Saturday mornings, my father would take my three siblings and me to the Parisian Bakery in Toronto. As he opened the door, the smell of freshly baked bread would envelop us like a warm blanket. We would have to have some of the bread my father had purchased even before we left the shop, while my father chatted with the baker. It was one of those regular family outings that remains forever fixed in my memory. Whenever I smell freshly baked bread, I immediately have the sensation of that little girl enjoying a Saturday morning with her sisters, brother, and father.

When I smell baby powder, that immediately reminds me of when my son was a baby – he had just had a bath, and I would cuddle with him in a rocking chair. My son is now a grown man, and yet that memory comes back to me whenever I smell baby powder and relive those moments. Music is another memory-jogger for me and other people as well. A certain song recalls a happy or sad moment, with a memory of when it happened and who was there. In fact, you can re-live that exact moment in your mind.

"Remember me," spoken by the ghost of Hamlet's father is uttered in an effort to encourage Hamlet to recreate and feel his dead father's pain, in order to maintain his resolve and do what he has to do.

Theorists argue whether cellular memory is real or not. However, the advocates insist that we maintain information on all levels of our being – physically, emotionally, mentally, and spiritually. Whether true or not, we do have the ability to remember complete details of specific events and our responses and can use that to our advantage.

What we do in this step of the process is to find that response. If you consciously remember an event, you can re-create it in your mind. By bringing all the senses into play, you can remember how you felt, what you could see, smell, hear, taste, and feel at that moment. Constantin Stanislavski's system was based on this sense memory.[17] Where you were at the time of the event, the other people involved, and the incidents leading up to the event all help to re-create the moment for you. Once that moment is re-created in its entirety, the next step is to intuitively find a word or gesture that conveys the moment to you. Actors need to experiment to determine what best works for them and for the character they are trying to portray. With practice, you are able to recall that moment and the related feelings or emotions by simply saying the word or doing the gesture. This was the internal part of the system – working from the "inside out" to create the emotions. This added to the physical actions – working from the "outside in" – allows the actor (and the businessperson) to be truly authentic in the role.

During the course of your day, business or personal, you're going to use different roles as required. You need to be able to call upon that role immediately. This step allows you to be immediately in that state, and more importantly, it allows you to be real.

Two factors required in business today – authenticity and speed. When you are genuine with people, they respond in kind. It leaves no room for second-guessing or mixed messages. Speed is essential in today's business world. When you can respond quickly and authentically in any situation, you have an enormous advantage. Clients, vendors, and colleagues all recognize it, whether consciously or not, and respond to it.

What happens, because you're able to call on this, you're certainly very authentic in your communication and it tends to be infectious – in a good way. It trickles throughout the organization. You're able to connect with people, you're able to connect with your co-workers, your supervisors, your staff, and that connection becomes much more valuable. With that, you become a much more competent and successful leader. I believe we are all leaders in today's business world. Every person, regardless of their position, in an organization has an opportunity to lead and make a difference. Using the theater analogy, everybody is important to the success of the play, whether onstage or behind the curtains. In business as well, every role is important to the success of the organization, and everyone is a leader in their particular step in the process. They all need to be as effective and efficient as possible in the moment.

We are all extremely unique. This step utilizes an individual's strengths. How wonderful to use your personal power, what is really you, rather than copying someone else. With this comes your passion in your communications, and that is very powerful. People respond to passion because they can feel the energy that comes with it. Do you know of a successful person who is not passionate about what they do? It motivates, encourages teamwork, engagement, and involvement in the success of the organization. It helps every level of the organization because everyone is motivating and inspiring each other.

Be the best you for the situation in an instant by remembering at all levels of your being when you were in an experience that required a particular role. By anchoring the memory and calling upon it as required, you are readily available to recreate that role whenever you choose.

"Nothing So Certain As Your Anchors"
The Winter's Tale – Act IV Scene IV

Immediate Adjustment

A s Shakespeare has Camillo comment in *The Winter's Tale*, "Nothing so certain as your anchors" – many sailors would concur. The anchor holds a ship in place, keeps it from drifting, and makes it readily available for you.

The third step in the process is ANCHOR. That means anchoring the character, holding the role that you have identified in place, and being able to call on that particular role immediately whenever you need it. The anchor can be a word or a gesture. Actors often use a gesture to get and keep them in character even while on stage. As an actor or a business person, you may not have time to think consciously about how you should be at a particular moment. Using your anchor allows you to "be" in that state immediately.

Those memories that we have, whether at the cellular level or not, are experiences that we have had, which we have full memory of, and can be used to our advantage. What happened in that experience and how we responded to it is very powerful. In a given situation, it may be critical to call upon a particular character to provide the best response. There may not be a lot of time to do that. By anchoring the response of the character, you can recall it immediately in an instant.

How can you do this? Having someone guide you through it makes it easier and more effective. However, you can do it yourself. Review the roles you have identified and recall moments in that role that were extremely positive and fulfilling. It doesn't have to be as a business person or even as an adult. For example, most of us have had moments in our lives when we were powerful, successful, and perhaps even viewed as a leader.

The next step is to recreate the memory as if it were occurring in the present. Sit in a quiet place with no distractions. (That means all digital devices off!) Recall the moment in as much detail as possible. Start with the external. Where are you? Are you inside or outside? What do you see? Why are you there? What are you wearing? Is it day or night? Are there other people around, or are you on your own? What is said or done to you or by you? What are you hearing? Do you taste anything? Do you smell anything? Are you touching anything? Describe each of these details in your mind as completely as possible. Then move to the internal. What are you thinking? What are you feeling? As you recreate this moment using all your senses and memories, it will be as if you are actually there. Immediately while in full recall, think of a word or gesture that symbolizes it for you. It should be the first word or gesture that comes to mind. That becomes your anchor.

Note in your workbook, in as much detail as possible, the sense memory you recreated and the anchor you chose. The process can be repeated for other roles and other memories, creating a different anchor for each of them.

Practice repeating the word or gesture and recreating the memory a number of times. Eventually, the word and gesture alone will put you in that state at all levels of your being. You will soon find that you can use it quickly to your advantage. For example, if you're about to make a presentation to a large number of people, and you are concerned with your impact on them, you can immediately bring yourself back to a moment of assuredness, of professionalism, of authority, and most importantly, of authenticity.

In business today, everything is much, much faster. So being able to anchor the role, call on it when needed, and be in the role immediately is very powerful.

With a little practice, you can bring yourself into that total state of being instantly and effortlessly by using the word or gesture. Your whole body will remember that sensation, that sensation of success or of happiness. Whatever it is that you want to use, you can bring it back instantly and use it in a particular situation. So that anchor word allows you to call on any role that you have experienced before and allows you to re-live it and be that role immediately. It becomes an almost unconscious response that is required for that situation.

It's phenomenal to see it in organizations when everybody is involved because it's immediately applicable. Someone can read the book and start working on it right way. They can start working on their roles. They can immediately start looking at how they project; they can get feedback in a safe environment. They can find that anchor word that allows them to be able to switch roles. It utilizes the individual's strengths, and with everyone in the organization doing the same, it strengthens the company as a whole.

ACT V SCENE I

"Action is Eloquence"

Coriolanus – Act III Scene II

Do it Every Day

How does an actor convincingly play the same role over and over again – eight performances a week, sometimes for years? Passion for his work certainly helps. Preparation plays an enormous part. Practice is what keeps him going week after week. Rehearsals are the initial steps, but the action of continuous practice of the character keeps him dedicated to the role.

How do you remain dedicated to the roles you have chosen? You have found your identities; you know how to project each one and have specifically anchored every characterization so that you can call on what you need easily at any time. What do you do next? How do you maximize your performance on an ongoing basis?

The last step in the process is DUPLICATE. Take what you know and do it. As with anything, start slowly, a little bit at a time. It's like having rehearsals and getting "off-book" (i.e., not using your script) more and more each time until you can do it with ease and with confidence.

This means change. You will be doing things a little differently. It's a process and with any process or change, it doesn't happen overnight. Do a little at a time and notice the results. An actor cannot walk out on opening night and give a brilliant and perfect performance without the many hours of work and practice beforehand. Often when learning their lines, directors will ask the ensemble to use a technique called "speed dialogue." It is simple. The entire cast sits around a table, and without an inflection or emphasis or emotion, recites all the lines as quickly as possible. This is to ensure that the cast is so comfortable with their dialogue that it would no longer inhibit the performance. When you are in your role, does what you say come naturally? As a leader, as a business person, could you really speed-dialogue through your character and know that you are authentic in your communications?

Let me give you an example of the process in action. I had a client who was CEO of an organization, and he came to me because he felt he just wasn't connecting with his people. He knew his business; he was personable and had a great team of people working for him. Something just didn't seem to be working. For some reason, when he got in front of his people, whether it was a group of people or just one-on-one, there just didn't seem to be any rapport. You might say he "had the steak but no sizzle."

We started working together and interestingly, in looking at his identities, he found within himself the role that was lacking. He had a sense that as a CEO, he had to walk around with a stern look on his face and be very serious all the time, making him actually very unapproachable. Often, in our roles, we use characteristics that have been put upon us, either through family, business, or friends. His concept of a leader was not who he authentically was, but what he thought he was supposed to be. In going through the process, he realized the role that he was playing wasn't really him, and it certainly wasn't effective for the company.

As he started to work through the process and make small changes, his people saw the differences and were a little bit surprised. It didn't happen overnight, but very gradually, he began to do things differently. At first, he started taking off his jacket when he walked around the office. Previously, he would always wear it because to him, that was a sign of a leader. People noticed. Then he learnt to smile a bit more which was difficult for him, because again, his impression of a leader was someone with a serious and stern look on his face. People smiled back. It was a gradual process, and each step made a difference in how he related to his people and they to him. His people would approach him with new ideas, and he responded well.

Gradually, he was able to change. He did not become great buddies with everybody in the organization, but when he walked around, he'd say good morning or good afternoon. If he saw a birthday card at someone's desk, he'd say, "Is it your birthday today? That's great – happy birthday." He learned to talk about the nice little things, not just business. Soon, some of the other roles that he played in his life, and not necessarily in business, began to emerge, and his concept of the role of a leader changed as well. When he started bringing those roles to the business world, it was amazing. He had a phenomenal rapport with his people, and it helped how his people worked with his customers. His customers found it a much better company to work with, and his business grew. It improved the bottom line. At the end of the day, that's what it's all about in business. Happy people do make happy businesses, and happy businesses are successful.

Let's take a look at some of the difficulties you might encounter as you roll this out. This is change, and often people resist change. This may appear in a variety of ways. Every actor at some time or another has worked with a "diva" – whether female or male – a person with a huge ego who thinks that he is the most important part of the show and that no one else matters. In her mind, everything rests on her shoulders. But even a one-person show has the much needed support of the backstage crew. Do you have any divas in your company? Do you have people who are so caught up in being stars that they forget that they're really working with other people? These people may well resist the change because they don't know how to handle this new way of communicating.

Some people may have suspicions about the change and be reluctant to accept the process. This could be based on previous personal experiences or some rumors that may be heard around the organization. This is all part of promoting the new process and indicates the need to handle any gossip quickly and positively.

Actors have a number of superstitions about their work. The most common one related to Shakespeare is that the play *Macbeth* is said to be cursed. Actors never mention the actual name but call it "The Scottish Play" instead. Interestingly, if an actor mistakenly mentions the name Macbeth while in the theater, she must leave the actual building, spin around outside three times, spit, curse, and then knock on the door to be allowed back into the building. This is a long-standing tradition based on the legend, that in the opening scene of the play, real witches were used to speak the incantations, which were said to be genuine. The legend continues that a witch cursed the play as revenge for revealing these secret spells. However, I don't suggest that you implement this particular technique in your rollout of this process.

Actors consider it bad luck to wish someone "good luck." Instead, they use the expression "break a leg," which is actually a wish that the performance will be so magnificent that the actor would have to break a leg – or bend at the knee – in a deep bow to acknowledge the thunderous applause.

To get that applause in your business, the process is simple. Start gradually and move step by step. IDENTIFY the particular character. Find that character, perhaps in movies or in theater, and see how they are portrayed. What is it about the character that makes you believe that they are who they are?

What are they doing to PROJECT that character? What is it about the way they talk or how they handle other people? Is there something about the character that attracts you? Is there something that you really like? Are there things that repel you, and if so, why? Is it because they're being too strong in what they're doing? Have they lost the authenticity in some way? Are they not truly being the character? Look around you and decide what it is that creates the character, not just for you, but how other people respond to it. People will see the character in you. They'll recognize it. They'll know that it's true. It's not false or fraudulent. They know who they're talking to whenever they have that communication with you.

Use the single word callback technique to ANCHOR the character. Use it to get yourself to the role and get there fast. Work with your anchor so that it is ingrained in you.

How do you move from who you are to your character? The same way that an actor does – DUPLICATE it. Practice in small ways. Walk like the character or talk like the character, and eventually, you'll start to be the character in everyday life.

Is it easy to do? For some people, it will be. For others, it may take more time. It will be important that you get out of your comfort zone. If you've always been another way, perhaps you've never been really and truly you. It is the real you, the character that you want to be. It simply takes focus and consciousness. If you work on it every single day, all the time, it finally becomes extremely natural, and finally, the true you is revealed and sustained.

ACT V SCENE II

"We Know What We Want But Know Not What We May Be"

Hamlet — Act IV Scene V

The Success of Your Business

The remarkable aspect of this process is that it is immediately applicable. You can start doing it right away. You can start working on your identities and become aware of what they are, when you use them, and when you can consciously choose to use them. You can observe how you project those identities. You can determine your anchor holds. And then, start to be the amazing "you" that you are every day. Once you're mindful of the roles and when you are using them in the course of the day, note what other thoughts are there. If you are truly being "in the moment," are you responding in a manner that belongs to a role that may not be appropriate for the current situation?

In order to practice this process and improve a little bit every day, one of the best things you can do is enroll others in your outcome. Initially, a trusted confidant who will be honest with you is a great ally to have. Just as actors work with their colleagues to create a character, working with another person will help you improve faster and be more effective. You might ask "How is this coming across to others?" or "What impression does this make on you?" It's the teamwork that is critical for each individual and for organizations as a whole.

As you move forward, enroll others and encourage them to work through the process. Enrollment is more than just talking someone into something. It's about connecting with that person in such a way that he or she is truly inspired and motivated to see what you see and buy into being part of it. Actors on stage enroll the audience in the story they are creating, and the audience lives through it with them. How often have you attended a play and totally forgotten that you were in the audience? That fourth wall disappears, and you are part of the events on stage. That's connection.

In an organization, it's important to enroll others so that they see how their purpose fits into the company's big picture. In order to make the connection with your people, it's important that the communication allows them to see that. If everyone in the company moved on purpose and was playing his or her role in the big picture, how would that company produce? When the individual's purpose is a part of the purpose of the organization and each other, you have a win-win.

Let me share a story with you. A question plagued me over and over again. Could I do it? It was two days before the end of the run of the performance, and I felt a sore throat coming on. I was doing everything to save my voice: not talking, using lozenges, and drinking warm water and honey. I made it through the second to last show; however, as I arrived at the theater on closing night, I realized that I was really starting to lose my voice. My biggest concern was the last scene. I had to let out a piercing scream that was critical to the plot. We were not using microphones, so I knew I had to get it to the back of the theater. I had convinced myself that I couldn't do it. I told my dear friend, another actor, my dilemma. The eternal optimist, she said not to worry. I would be fine, and I would get the scream to the back row. As the play progressed and my scream scene drew near, I forced myself to believe I could do it, but every time I spoke, my voice was getting raspier and raspier.

As actors, we sometimes become so caught up in our character, in being present with it, that we forget that we are not in it alone. There is a lot of help available. We forget or choose not to ask for that help. We were minutes from my scream. There was my cue. I opened my mouth...and a blood-curdling scream blew past me from the curtain directly behind me. My dear friend had positioned herself to be as close to me off-stage as she could, and she screamed for me. Sometimes, you ask for help. Sometimes, you don't. And sometimes, it just shows up.

Often, leaders don't get this. It's not just talking at your people and not just communicating, no matter how passionate you may be. You can have all the passion in the world, but if no one else is on board, if people are not enrolled, nothing will happen. That is the situation in so many organizations today in the corporate world. People may participate, but not to the extent and not to the level of success the leaders are looking to achieve. It's important to truly enroll them in the corporate vision. It's important to truly connect with them, no matter if you are presenting from the platform, if you are talking to the board, or if you are talking to individuals one-on-one. You need to have that connection. You need to enroll them in what you are trying to accomplish. It's all about enrolling the people and insuring that everyone on the team is fulfilling their own unique purpose. They have to see their purpose in the role they play and show up every day passionate about what they're going to do. It's imperative the leaders communicate better, to have their passion for the organization felt by their people and for their people to be enrolled in it. Let's face it. There may be individuals who are working at something that isn't their highest choice and isn't what they really want to do. After all, sometimes you simply need a job.

How can you motivate these people who may not be doing what they really want to do to be the best that they can be at what they are doing? Truly connecting with them in every possible communication. A true connection will enroll the people in what you see as your plan for the company and help them be a part of it.

As others join in, there is power in numbers. When you can get everybody on board, everybody thinking and working the same way, you have a powerful force that launches success. It will improve the efficiency of your organization, because again, everyone is working toward the same goal. Teamwork will improve. Productivity will improve. You'll have a much happier workforce. Practice it every single day – each individual in the organization practicing it in their communications and connecting effectively and authentically. After all, as the theater saying goes – "How do you get to Carnegie Hall? Practice, practice, practice."

What happens if everyone is not on board? I saw this happen in an organization where everyone was participating except for one vice president. He thought it was a load of rubbish, and he was just not going to be involved. What followed was most interesting. His colleagues started to see the characteristics of the role he was portraying and realized that was the way he conducted himself in business all the time. It was his way or no way. People found they were reluctant to work with him, and the results could have been severely critical for the company. Needless to say, he was quickly fired.

You start to realize that you may have been using these roles unconsciously. With this process, you will start to use it consciously, and you will be much more mindful of it. You'll start to listen to people more; you'll be in the moment and deal with what it is you have to deal with. You'll use the right role at the right time, and that is an enormous step towards your success.

A few things to keep in mind as you work through this process. First of all, you are unique. Who you are is absolutely wonderful. Celebrate who you are. Be honest and open and authentic with everyone around you. Secondly, change is never easy – it appears simple, it's not necessarily easy, but it's something that you can do, and in most cases, something you really should do. All of us can improve. Thirdly, any change has to happen in progression. One step at a time. You're not going to be wonderful overnight in the same way an actor doesn't learn his role overnight. It takes practice, practice, practice. Be willing to put in the time, be willing to practice, and be the absolute best "you" that you can be.

Let's take a look at some of the results you will experience. First of all and most importantly, the bottom line of the organization would be improved. Leaders would communicate with integrity and candor, both among themselves and with their people, and that would eventually evolve to employees communicating with each other – with their peers. Within the organization, you would know that people would be speaking with authenticity and honesty. There would be no second-guessing of what was going on – no hidden messages. You know how time-consuming that can be. You say to yourself, "What are they really saying? Do they mean that or do they mean this?" You know that if you hear something and know it is straightforward and honest, you can respond from your honesty.

I believe that today in the corporate world, people have stopped trusting. If you think someone has a hidden agenda, then you come from your hidden agenda, and the whole thing becomes very contrived and very false. But if you know that the person is speaking with honesty, you respond with honesty, and a lot more gets accomplished a lot faster. I believe the productivity of each employee would improve, which would eventually translate to a bottom-line improvement as well.

Secondly, the employees would be passionate, enrolled, and fulfilled and would realize their role in the organization. I mentioned earlier that the Gallup survey found that 87% of the workforce are not engaged in their jobs.[18] A recent article from Forbes reported that it costs the USA an estimated $300 billion – that's with a "b" – $300 billion per year in treatment for stress-related problems, absenteeism, reduced productivity, and employee turnover.[19] How could we radically shift that number? What if people were passionate about what they were doing? What if people felt less stress and were more excited to come to work?

Every employee would feel connected in the big vision and know their part in creating and maintaining it. People would be closer to their own passion, so they could give 110%. On a day-to-day basis, when people are passionate about what they are doing, they do it the best they can. They work more efficiently because they know they are making a contribution. They are coming up with possible new ideas for improvements because they know in the end it is something good for them and how they do their job. They know that management and leadership are open to suggestions. With every employee producing at peak performance, this would instantaneously improve the bottom line. When you and your position are a perfect fit, it's magic. And the rest is easy.

Thirdly, can you imagine being a client or a customer of an organization like this? What would it be like doing business with people who are all communicating and connecting and doing business with people who want you, the client, to have a memorable experience with them and their company? Do you think you would feel good doing business with these people? Do you think you as the client would build a relationship and have loyalty to the organization? Absolutely. People at all levels would be exceeding expectations because they would be in tune with the organization. It's like the play you go to where you come out singing one of the songs you heard. You are remembering the message.

That's what it is – creating a company that is prosperous and productive; you have people who are on purpose, people who love to come to work, who know that they are making a contribution, know that they are an integral part of the organization, and not just simply workers there. Just think of it: people connecting with people, improved communications leader-to-leader, and leaders to their people, employees to each other, employees to the customer. It's magnificent. You have a company with a productive work environment, an improved bottom line, passionate and involved employees, and happy, loyal clients.

To this date, the longest-running musical performed in the USA is Broadway's *Phantom of the Opera,* which opened on January 26, 1988. The longest-running musical play in the world is *Les Misérables,* having opened in London's West End on October 8, 1985. And the longest-running play in the world, *The Mousetrap,* opened in London's West End on November 25, 1952. That's 26, 28, and 61 years respectively!

Longevity results from a job well done. You can have a hit company. And just like a hit play, it continues on forever.

Encore

The Ghost Light

There is a theatrical superstition that a theater must never be left completely dark or ghosts would take up residence. This would include good ghosts of past performances at the theater who would return to the stage to live out their brilliant moments. It would also include bad ghosts who want to create havoc in the theater. To prevent this, a single bare bulb on a wire frame and mounted on a portable stand is left burning at center stage. It is lit by the last person to leave the theater after the audience and all of the actors, musicians, and stage crew have gone.

The origin of this superstition has both practical and further superstitious aspects to it. A darkened theater is a dangerous place where delicate costumes, sharp props, and heavy set pieces have been left lying about. The practicality is the light is necessary to prevent injury, property damage, and possible lawsuits.

The other reason advances further superstition. A "dark" theater is a theater without a play whether due to lack of funding or even worse an unsuccessful production that was forced to close. An empty house and a play-less stage is devastating to a drama artist. Therefore, the ghost light burning center stage ensures the theater is never "dark."

It is simply awaiting the next production.

Keep your light on!

Get out there and break a leg!

About the Author

Linda Sherwin has over 20 years of extensive experience in both corporate training/coaching and performance in domestic and international markets. She works with leaders in a broad spectrum of industries in both the public and private sector to help them connect and communicate with confidence to improve productivity and performance in their organizations. Her unique sessions and readily applicable techniques make her a much sought-after resource.

Known for her passionate presentation style and high energy, Linda teaches her clients how to tap into their own personal effectiveness to increase productivity, attract loyal customers, retain involved employees, and improve the bottom line by encouraging authentic communication at all levels of the organization.

With the experience and know-how of a corporate consultant and the highly developed presentation skills of a professional performer, Linda uses theatrical techniques that create award-winning performances on stage and translates them into a communication method for use in the world of business. She has delivered keynotes, seminars, workshops, and coaching sessions on the impact of full communications in all areas of business and life.

Here for the first time, Linda presents these highly successful techniques in written format for the world!

Reference Notes

1. Larson, Jonathan. (1996). *Seasons of Love* [Original Broadway Cast]. On *Rent: Original Broadway Cast Recording* [Album]. New York, New York. Accessed on September 2, 2013

2. "State of the Global Workplace Report 2013," Gallup, accessed October 21, 2013, http://www.gallup.com/strategicconsulting/164735/state-global-workplace.aspx

3. Adams, Susan, November 11, 2011 (12:16 p.m.). "Employee Loyalty Dropping Worldwide," Forbes, accessed August 9, 2013, http://www.forbes.com/sites/susanadams/2011/11/10/employee-loyalty-dropping-worldwide/

4. "Build a Better Workplace: Employee Engagement Edition," Ipsos Reid for Canadian Management Centre, August 2012, accessed August 9, 2013, http://www.ipsos.ca/common/dl/pdf/research/loyalty/IpsosLoyalty-BetterWorkplace.pdf

5. National Science Foundation, http://www.nsf.gov

6. Peters, John Durham. (1999). *Speaking into the air: A history of the idea of communication*. Chicago, IL: University of Chicago Press, 7, accessed July 9, 2013 http://www.colorado.edu/communication/meta-discourses/Theory/latin.htm

7. Mehrabian, Albert. (1971). *Silent Messages* (1st ed.). Belmont, CA: Wadsworth.

8. Betts, Kristen. (2009). "Lost in Translation: Importance of Effective Communication in Online Education," Online Journal of Distance Learning Administration, Volume XII, Number II, Summer 2009, University of West Georgia, Distance Education Center, accessed July 10, 2013 http://www.westga.edu/~distance/ojdla/summer122/betts 122.html

9. "Build a Better Workplace: Employee Engagement Edition," Ipsos Reid for Canadian Management Centre, August 2012, accessed August 9, 2013, http://www.ipsos.ca/common/dl/pdf/research/loyalty/Ipso sLoyalty-BetterWorkplace.pdf

10. Wargo, Eric. (2006). "How Many Seconds to a First Impression?," Association for Psychological Science, Observer Vol. 19, No. 7 July, 2006, accessed on July 9, 2013 https://www.psychologicalscience.org/index.php/publicatio ns/observer/2006/july-06/how-many-seconds-to-a-first-impression.html

11. Goman, Carol Kinsey, February 13, 2011 (12:14 p.m.). "Seven Seconds to Make a First Impression," Forbes, accessed July 10, 2013, http://www.forbes.com/sites/carolkinseygoman/2011/02/1 3/seven-seconds-to-make-a-first-impression/ based on Schiller, D., Freeman, J.B., Mitchell, J.P., Uleman, J.S., and Phelps, E.A., "A neural mechanism of first impressions," 8 March 2009, *Nature Neuroscience* 12, 508-514 doi:10.1038/nn.2278, http://www.stanford.edu/group/ipc/pubs/2009Schiller.pdf

12. Stanislavski, Constantin. (1936). *An Actor Prepares*. London: Methuen, 1988.

13. Hullar, Timothy E. (2009). "Why Does My Voice Sound So Different When It is Recorded Back," Scientific American: Mind & Brain Ask the Experts, accessed July 9, 2013 http://www.scientificamerican.com/article/why-does-my-voice-sound-different/

14. Haggard, Ernest A. & Isaacs, Kenneth S. (1966). *Micromomentary facial expressions as indicators of ego mechanisms in psychotherapy.* In L.A. Gottschalk & A.H. Auerback (Eds.), *Methods of research in psychotherapy.* New York: Appleton-Centuru-Crofts.

15. Ekman, Paul. (1985). *Telling Lies: Clues to Deceit in the Marketplace, Politics and Marriage.* New York: W.W. Norton & Co.

16. Eisenberg, Anne. "When Algorithms Grow Accustomed to Your Face," *New York Times,* December 1, 2013, accessed December 1, 2013, http://www.nytimes.com/2013/12/01/technology/when-algorithms-grow-accustomed-to-your-face.html?_r=0

17. Stanislavski, Constantin. (1936). *An Actor Prepares.* London: Methuen, 1988.

18. "State of the Global Workplace Report 2013," Gallup, accessed October 21, 2013, http://www.gallup.com/strategicconsulting/164735/state-global-workplace.aspx

19. "Wakeman, Cy, June 20, 2013, (9:06 a.m.). "The Source of Your Stress," Forbes, accessed July 10, 2013, http://www.forbes.com/sites/cywakeman/2013/06/20/the-source-of-your-stress/